Successful Master Planning

Successful Master Planning

More than Pretty Pictures

Timothy L. Cool

iUniverse, Inc.
New York   Bloomington

Successful Master Planning
More than Pretty Pictures

iUniverse books may be ordered through booksellers or by contacting:

iUniverse
1663 Liberty Drive
Bloomington, IN 47403
www.iuniverse.com
1-800-Authors (1-800-288-4677)

ISBN: 978-1-4502-2197-9 (sc)
ISBN: 978-1-4502-2195-5 (dj)
ISBN: 978-1-4502-2196-2 (ebk)

Printed in the United States of America

iUniverse rev. date: 04/07/2010

Contents

Foreword

Let's face it: for the most part, pastors are not trained to do the things we are most often required to do.

We are well-schooled in studying and teaching from the Bible, helping people navigate crisis moments in their lives, and caring for souls. We can put together a credible Christian education program and help develop new believers into committed disciples. All of these things are important, central to our calling.

But it is rare that we are trained in other important things we must do: crafting guiding values for our churches, putting an effective performance review process in place, setting sound financial policy, and making sure our facilities are maintained well. One challenge in particular is important: crafting a compelling, guiding vision.

Oh, we are pretty good visionaries. We can *see* the buildings and how they will enhance our ministry and transform our communities. But often the process of getting them planned, designed, and built feels mysterious and intimidating.

An intelligent master plan process is an essential part of a successful building program. The process is a serious one that requires diligence and patience, and it often takes more time than we assume. Creating a master plan the right way can bring unity, a renewed sense of purpose, and financial stability to our churches. Failing to plan can kill momentum, sow division, and result in financial crises.

Fortunately, church leaders now have a comprehensive primer for the master planning process. Tim Cool's *Successful Master Planning: More Than Pretty Pictures* is a realistic, helpful, and liberating overview of this all-important process. Packed with practical application, Tim's work can help every church leader lead more effectively and wisely through a building program.

Tim is the right guy to write this book. He has helped over two hundred churches in his career and has become one of the most sought-after experts in the United States for helping churches manage growth and organization challenges. He has real-world experience as an executive in a national church building organization.

Plus, he *gets* churches. Tim and I helped start a new church together, so I know firsthand his commitment to the local church and its people.

If you are considering a building program, are in the middle of one, or think you might consider one many years down the road, then reading Tim's wise and helpful book will be a great investment of your time.

Todd Hahn
Lead Pastor
Next Level Church
Charlotte, NC

Introduction

M eet Pastor Bob. He is the pastor of First Presbyterian Church of somewhere, anywhere, everywhere. His church is not just Presbyterian, but also Baptist, Methodist, Episcopal, Lutheran, Nazarene, Independent, and so on and so forth. In short, he is my pastor and your pastor. He is my father, who was a Wesleyan pastor for over twenty-five years. He represents any leader of a church or ministry who has or ever will consider a facilities expansion or building program. He is the embodiment of every person who has led a growing organization and who has felt a leading from the Lord to explore how physical facilities may serve as a tool to further the growth, influence, and ministry of the church.

I have spent the past twenty-three years working with "Bobs" and their teams to navigate the rough waters of facilities expansion projects across the United States. I worked with these ministries to navigate issues related to land and site selection, zoning and re-zoning, master planning, architectural review processes, schematic design coordination, construction document coordination, value engineering, funding and financing, construction, post-construction, and just about everything in between. During that time I was blessed to serve over two hundred ministries, helping to explore and implement their facility needs and wants.

Many of these projects required significant prayer and soul-searching to determine the real needs and motivations behind such an endeavor. I have worked with many "Bobs" who have huge vision; it was sometimes unrealistic, but at least they had vision. In those cases we had to take the time to dive deep into the issues associated with the vision as well as the significant aspects of financial capability and practicality of the vision.

These were not always pleasant processes, but when the church was willing to invest the time, energies and resources to work through them, the results were remarkable. Not only did I witness churches making the right choice for their situation, but I also saw hearts melted, saw visions set on fire by the passion and the coming together of God's people for a united purpose. This is what drives me, what keeps me up at night, what makes me crazy at times.

But my passion is not drawing plans, digging dirt, building buildings, or maintaining completed structures. What I am passionate about is assisting churches, ministries, and their leadership to be true stewards of the things with which God has entrusted them, which include but are not limited to dollars, buildings, people, and ministry opportunities.

The master planning process is not merely a formal exercise to add more meetings to an already-busy church calendar; it is the foundation of any expansion program. This process must not be passed-over or short-circuited. The data you develop will serve you and your team well now and long into the future.

There are a lot of perils in a master planning process. Your dream can get derailed if your facilities vision is too grandiose.

People far from God who could have been reached by your ministry will remain far from God as a result. Families who could have been knit back together at your church will remain in conflict because you were not able to build important facilities. Your church could struggle to remain unified and focused because of financial bondage. To be sure, the stakes are high.

As you make your way through this book, you will find not only the theory behind master planning, but also some very practical tools to help apply the principles to your specific church and ministry. In the Appendices you will find some "worksheets" for you to use with your team as a guide to develop some preliminary plans.

Prologue:

Pastor Bob's Frustration

"Would you tell me which way I ought to go from here?" asked Alice.
"That depends a good deal on where you want to get," said the Cat.
"I really don't care where," replied Alice.
"Then it doesn't much matter which way you go," said the Cat.

—*Alice In Wonderland* by Lewis Carroll

It had been another frustrating meeting, one in a series of frustrating meetings, and Pastor Bob was exhausted.

Now into his third year as pastor of First Presbyterian Church, Bob had inherited the leadership of a historic church that was experiencing a spurt of new life as its downtown location was beginning to attract young professionals and families. Bob—a gifted communicator and a people-person—was well-loved by his congregation; they had been responsive to his efforts to launch new ministries to reach their rapidly changing community, and the church had experienced significant growth in the last two years.

So much growth, in fact, that First Presbyterian was fast running out of space. They needed more room for the children's ministry and an expansion of the church offices, and they wanted to update their youth building and historic sanctuary.

At least, that was what Bob thought.

So he assembled a team of congregational leaders to help him turn his dreams into reality and to ensure that First Presbyterian would be able to meet the needs of the many new families with kids and teenagers who were coming to check the church out. The team included contractors, engineers, bankers, and gifted managers. Bob assumed he had a dream team that would help him navigate the planning, design, building, and financial challenges of the upcoming projects. His job, he assumed, was to explain the challenges facing the church, articulate his very clear vision for the church's next twenty years, and then let the experts bring it all to pass.

Only, it had not been quite that easy. Or easy at all, as a matter of fact.

The architects and engineers squabbled. The pastoral staff all insisted that the physical needs of their individual ministry areas had to take center stage. The bankers seemed to delight in throwing a financial wet blanket over every hot, visionary idea Bob came up with.

Bob got into the habit of taking a small bottle of Advil to the project team meetings.

After one particularly contentious meeting, Bob trudged back toward his office to gather his briefcase and coat and make the weary drive home. As he left the building, Tom, one of the project team members, asked if he could walk with Pastor Bob to his car. Bob agreed.

"Pastor," Tom began, "I can't help but notice that you seem to be really discouraged by this process. Is there anything I can do to help?" Encouraged by a caring question from someone not fighting for turf or shooting down ideas, Bob opened up, surprising even himself.

"Tom," he replied, "I am beyond discouraged. I am getting downright depressed. I never knew that this process was going to be so agonizing. This church has had great unity; the people are wonderful; we are growing. I assumed this building project would be like everything else in the last three years—challenging, but exciting and fun. After all, 'God's work, God's way,' right?"

Bob tossed his briefcase into the backseat and sighed wearily. "Gotta be honest with you, though; I figured that at this point we would have some pretty pictures to show the congregation. You know, cool color drawings, small-scale models of new buildings in the vestibule. I thought my job was just to articulate the vision, to say what needed to be done, and then together we would figure out how to design it, build it, and pay for it. That's a master plan, right? That's what I need: a master plan. Now I am wondering if I need a combination MBA, commercial contractor's license, and architecture degree just to make any sense of this!"

Bob sighed and shook Tom's hand. "Thanks for asking, Tom. Now I've got to get home to the kids." He started to put his key in the ignition, paused, and turned back to his friend. "You know, I just did not know a building project would be this hard and discouraging. I am not even sure I have what it takes to lead First Presbyterian through this."

Pastor Bob started his car and drove off into the night.

Chapter One:

The Journey Begins

"Plans are only good intentions unless they immediately degenerate into hard work."

— Peter Drucker

W hen Pastor Bob said, "I need a master plan," what he really meant was, "I need to have a concrete vision of the future so that I can cast vision and so that we can raise the needed resources to accomplish our ministry." Both goals are worthy ones and a good Master Planning process will make them possible. However, like most leaders, Pastor Bob did not fully understand the complexity of the process. In particular, he underestimated the sheer amount of data that must be gathered, evaluated, and processed before a clear picture of the future can emerge.

Simply put, Bob is not exactly sure what master planning actually is. In this, he is not alone. I am writing this book to help leaders just like Bob have clarity and confidence when it comes to navigating the master-planning process. Let's start with a working definition.

Our definition incorporates three dimensions:

1. A programmatic study of current and long-range ministry plans, and how facilities may or may not assist in accomplishing those plans.
2. A vision of the future, beginning with today's realities.
3. A clear, big-picture view of the ministry's future based upon consideration of a ministry's needs, hopes, and desires.

Let's look at each of these dimensions in turn.

A Programmatic Study

A master plan, by definition, requires a thorough approach. In order to analyze a ministry's situation, the planners must collect data, carry out research, perform due diligence, and ask lots of pointed questions. It is impossible to plan wisely without a comprehensive review of a ministry's current resources, desires, and capabilities.

Let's say that our family agrees that it is time for us to take a vacation. We are all in agreement that we need a break, but that is where the consensus ends. We're not sure where to go, what we should do when we get there, when we should depart and return, and how much money we should spend. We need to do extensive research, seek the input of the involved parties and consider their desires and needs, and review our available resources in order to set a budget and take our kids desires and needs into consideration.

My wife and I consult our "cherubs" (they are not always "angels" by any stretch!), dive into the process, and come up with these initial findings:

1. We want to go to the mountains. We love the mountains and even hope to live there one day. We could go to the beach, to a large city, or to an amusement park but, for this vacation, the mountains are the right choice.
2. We want to stay for a week. Any less time and we will not be fully rested and rejuvenated. Any longer and we would start to get on each other's nerves.
3. We have arrived at a feasible dollar amount for our trip budget. We know how much cash we have on hand and how much we are willing to finance with credit cards.

So, are we are ready to leave? Not quite. We still have some very important questions to answer. Consider the following:

1. Which mountains?
2. Do we want to stay in a log cabin, a house, a condo, a hotel, a camper, or a tent?
3. Which week is the best, based on any potential conflicts with our family's schedule of school, sports, church activities, lessons?
4. How much vacation time do we have available from work?
5. How much of our available resources should we allocate for lodging? For gas? Food? Entertainment? How much should we keep in reserve in case of an emergency?

Once we've answered all these, it must be time to pack the car, right? Almost—but we still have more research to do!

This next phase of planning the trip is the most challenging. This is where wishes and desires come face to face with reality. It is the moment of compromise.

We would love to stay at a five-star resort with a full day-spa and all the amenities, but our budget will allow only an RV or condo. My wife and I would love to dine out for every meal in four-star restaurants, but our budget says only one restaurant meal per day. The kids would be thrilled to experience the amusement parks or the "zip line" or

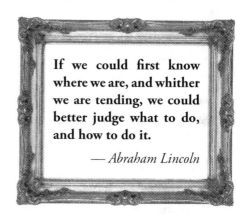

If we could first know where we are, and whither we are tending, we could better judge what to do, and how to do it.

— *Abraham Lincoln*

activities that require an extra fee, but in reality, hiking at the national park and swimming in the lake are all that we can afford.

You have probably planned family vacations in a similar manner; such preparation is second nature for most of us. For some reason, however, ministries tend to skip over this sort of research. Without the strong foundation laid by this study phase, ministries can flounder and encounter severe financial challenges.

A Future Vision Based on Today's Realities

The second dimension of master planning involves a vision of the future firmly rooted in the realities of today. Let's stick with our vacation analogy for a moment. The vision of our mountain getaway that is beginning to emerge is based solidly on an honest assessment of our current realities. For example:

1. We assume everyone is going to be healthy. If someone gets sick, the whole vacation could have to be canceled or postponed.
2. We assume that the price of gasoline will remain fairly consistent. If there is a 20- or 30-percent spike in gas costs, the entire trip could come into question
3. We assume the family car is roadworthy (we even plan to have it serviced before we leave). If we have a flat tire or an accident, it could throw off our budget and the timing of the vacation.
4. We assume our lodging reservations will be honored. If there is a mix-up, or a fire, or the hotel goes out of business, could we easily find other available accommodations at an affordable price? Or would we have to rethink all of our plans?

This list, of course, is not complete. There are many other issues that could arise.

Master planning is, of course, about the future—and the future is inherently unpredictable. Experienced planners don't have crystal balls enabling us to predict the future with absolute certainty. Instead, we include contingency plans, taking into account the "what if?" questions. This does not mean we are pessimistic or frightened. It simply means we are honest and prudent.

A Big Picture View of the Future
We are nearly ready to pack the car and head to the mountains, where the air is crisp and the temperature is twenty degrees cooler! Before the garage door goes up, however, we have one more

dimension of our plan to consider: the specific details that will finish the picture of our vacation painted in broad strokes.

Where will we eat when we splurge on a restaurant, and what sorts of meals will we cook at home? Where will we stop along the way? What sites do we want to make sure we don't miss? What do we hope our vacation does for our family relationally, spiritually, and emotionally?

A good master plan, like a good vacation, requires a lot of preparation, thought, research, contingency planning, and discussion. A bad vacation features empty wallets, late arrivals, unplanned-for crises, and a grumpy family. A bad master plan can result in frustrated expectations, financial shortfalls, divided leadership, and decades of regret. The rest of this book will show you how to prevent such a disaster from distracting or derailing your ministry. Let's head for the mountains!

Chapter Two:

From the Inside Out

"Suppose one of you wants to build a tower. Will he not first sit down and estimate the cost to see if he has enough money to complete it? For if he lays the foundation and is not able to finish it, everyone who sees it will ridicule him, saying, 'This fellow began to build and was not able to finish.'"

— *Jesus Christ (Luke 14:28–30)*

In my many years working with churches, I have sadly had to watch more than once as a promising master planning process becomes a train wreck. At the beginning, there is a sense of excitement; possibilities for the future seem limitless. The ministry leaders genuinely want to serve God, and people are full of enthusiasm. Then something goes wrong. Friends are at odds; a project is dramatically over budget; ministry dreams slowly die.

More often than not, this happens when a ministry shortchanges the first, and most crucial, part of the master planning process: the programmatic collection of data through disciplined research. This information concerns opportunities, resources, and challenges within the organization itself. We *have* to start from the inside out. Over the years, I have come to see that there are six critical questions that must be asked, answered, and analyzed by all involved in the master planning process:

1. What is the vision of our ministry?
2. Who is our "target market"?
3. What is our DNA as a ministry?
4. What do we consider to be "value"?
5. If space and finances were not an issue, what ministries would we start or enlarge?
6. If we do not start or enlarge the above ministries, what kind of impact will that decision have on our overall ministry, community and vision?

Let's explore each of these critical questions.

1. What is the vision of your ministry?

The two key words in this question are "vision" and "your." They are specific and personal to your ministry. The vision is where you, as the leader(s) of the ministry, believe that God wants you to take His work.

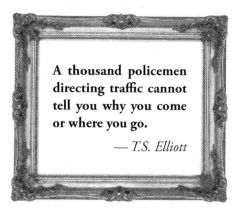

A thousand policemen directing traffic cannot tell you why you come or where you go.

— *T.S. Elliott*

And this must be your vision. No one else can tell you what your vision should be. No architect, builder, consultant, or friend can tell you what *your* vision is—the unique one that God has given to you. The team that you assemble to assist you through this process can help you decipher how that vision affects the material world implementation (facilities, land development, and so forth), but they cannot determine God's vision for your ministry; God gives that vision to the leader. Of course, a wise leader will seek input from wise and trusted counselors, but it is up to the leader to defend and articulate God's vision.

What is *your* vision for the ministry? Where do you see God leading you this year? Next year? Five, ten years from now?

If you can clearly articulate the vision and make it personal, then you are ready to gather more data. If you can't, you should turn to God and seek his vision; not until then can you marshal your leadership to pray and to dream big dreams. You might find that professional strategic consulting and planning will help at this juncture.

2. What is our target market?

For some, talk of churches having a "target market" is crass. After all, isn't our message for all people? Isn't targeting a certain market a secular pursuit unworthy of the Gospel of Christ? Isn't our job to take the good word to *all* people, not just a niche audience?

Please don't misunderstand. I am not suggesting that we forgo the Great Commission or that we don't care about certain groups of people. Keep in mind that the idea of a target market is not outside biblical parameters. Consider Paul. Paul's mission was to share the word of the saving grace provided to us through a personal relationship with Jesus Christ. As we study Paul's letters, we see that he understood each audience he addressed, and was able to tailor his message to their needs without ever changing the truth of the gospel. While his message didn't vary, Paul addressed the Greeks differently than he did Jews. Why? Because the Greeks and Jews were different "target market"; each had different backgrounds and foundations, and needed to be addressed in a manner that considered that.

Today, every church has a target market, whether or not the church thinks in those terms. My parents come from a traditional background and appreciate a worship setting with pews, hymnals, a pastor in a suit and tie, and a Sunday School program. They seek a fellowship of believers who subscribe to those same desires and values. I am thankful that they have found a church whose ministries "target" these desires. Many people, of all ages and backgrounds, share their preferences.

On the other hand, my family attends a church with a target very different from my parent's church. Our pastor wears jeans and t-shirts and we dress in shorts and flip-flops; we enjoy chest pounding, heart pumping, "rock-and-roll" worship with a congregation whose average age is much younger than that of many other churches in the area.

So recognize your target. What kind of person do you reach most effectively? What are the demographics of your community? Who is already sitting in your congregation, and what does that mean to your programs and methodologies and even staffing? Are your ministries and philosophy of worship the best to reach this target? Before moving on, it is important that you wrestle with these questions, perhaps with your leadership team. At times the discussion may be tough, but the emerging clarity will be worth it!

3. What is our DNA?

If you watch any popular television show dealing with forensic science and police work, you are certain to hear the term "DNA." The *American Heritage New Dictionary of Cultural Literacy*, third edition, defines DNA as "the molecule that carries information in all living systems."

In short, DNA is the molecular component that identifies each living being specifically, coding the biological components that make each of us unique. No two 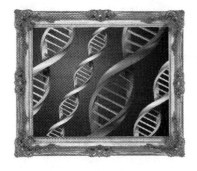 people have the exact same DNA. This also applies to ministry organizations as well: there are no two ministries exactly alike. There may be similarities, but there are still differences, even if they are only subtle.

So what is your ministry's DNA? What makes you unique from every other ministry in the world? What are your "molecular" markers? If your ministry were a cell and we put it under a microscope side by side with other cells, what would set you apart and make you unique?

1. Is your focus a multi-site ministry location?
2. Do you believe that a return to biblical orthodoxy is your most important priority?
3. Is urban ministry the differentiator?
4. Do you have a food pantry for the needy that drives your ministries?
5. Do you focus on small groups? If so, what sort of small-groups philosophy do you embrace?

You must decode your DNA and find out if that DNA aligns with your vision and target. If you are acting in a way not consistent with your DNA, your vision for the future of your ministry will prove difficult, if not impossible, to reach.

4. How do we define "value" for our ministry?

"Value" is an increasingly popular term in the business world, although it does not mean the same thing to all who use it. Some people think of value as synonymous with cost. Others equate value with great worth, such as a relationship or a prized possession. Many use the term "value-added," which refers to an extra quality of a service or product that you may not be paying for directly.

What does your ministry value as far as your physical facility is concerned? This will be a specific thing or group of things that you, as a leader, believe brings great worth or meaning to *your* ministry. Does your ministry value stained-glass windows and soaring beamed ceilings, or does it value the ability to get the most possible square footage at the least possible cost, regardless of the aesthetics? Perhaps your ministry values a large choir and great acoustics, or a cozy schoolroom where the youngest members gather for children's Bible study. Whatever you choose as your value priority, recognize that this commitment will shape the course of your master plan in profound ways.

The value question is related to your message; what do you want your ministry to "say" to the community God has given you? Spreading your message is not merely a verbal act. The way you allocate your resources, the appearance and design of your physical plant, your choices about community involvement—these are all ways of sharing what is most important to you.

It is particularly important that your budget be aligned with your values. Take a look at your church budget and your spending to date in order to examine if the way you spend the resources God has given you matches your message. Are you investing these funds in the areas that will help you minister to the target market God has given you the

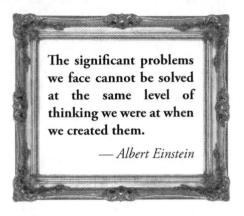

The significant problems we face cannot be solved at the same level of thinking we were at when we created them.

— *Albert Einstein*

passion to reach? If not—stop! A prerequisite to effective ministry is congruence at every level; you must bring the vision, target, DNA, values, and message into alignment with every choice you make.

While the first four questions require us to dig deep into who we believe God has called us to be, the next two questions start to address the desires of our hearts and the passions that motivates us.

5. If space and finances were not an issue, what ministries would you start or expand?

If you had all of the physical space you could ever want and an unlimited budget, what ministries would you enlarge? What new endeavors would you like to start? What would it take to make them a reality? How much space would it take? How many staff/ volunteers? How long would it take to implement?

This is the part of the process where you get to dream. Remember, a master plan is a "big picture" process. Ask all of your senior leadership and individual ministry leaders the questions

I have listed above. You may be surprised at the passion and creativity that can flow from people's hearts once they are given the opportunity to express themselves. However, remember that this part of the process must still

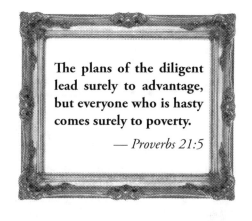

The plans of the diligent lead surely to advantage, but everyone who is hasty comes surely to poverty.

— *Proverbs 21:5*

come into alignment with your responses to the first four questions. Your dreaming must harmonize with your vision, target, DNA, and values; therefore, your discussion of the responses to this question must fall within those parameters, or you will run the risk of derailing the master planning process.

6. If you do *not* start or expand the above ministries, what kind of impact will it have on your community?

This is the most subjective of all of our questions, which may make it the most challenging. To answer it, you will have to indulge in a bit of speculation about what might happen if your ministry fails to enhance or create the ministries you envision as your goal. If we believe that our vision, target, and DNA are all aligned with our understanding of what God is leading us to do, and we are not able to accomplish these things, then what is the impact? What are the opportunities lost?

These are eternal questions, not merely part of a business plan. We are talking about people's lives and spiritual development; it is important that we find the best and most thorough way to affect and influence the lives of those whom God has called us to reach. This is a serious matter—one that, I know, you do not take lightly.

The master planning process begins when we answer these questions with honesty and courage. I mean courage in the literal sense; it is frightening to dig beneath the surface and unearth issues that are uncomfortable and possibly threatening. It is always easier to maintain the status quo than to wrestle with understanding our values and beliefs. Being a ministry leader is a hard enough calling; why invite the pain of a possible disagreement over philosophy and values?

However, I want to challenge you to consider what would have happened if Jesus had chosen to go with the flow rather than to confront the most important issues at hand. What if Saul had not followed Christ, changed his name to Paul, and ruffled more than a few feathers? What if Moses had come down from the mountain and said, "I know I have met with God and he has given me these great commandments but, hey, the people are so happy worshipping these idols ... why should I rock the boat?"

As the church of Jesus Christ, we do not have the luxury of going with the flow or maintaining the status quo. We have been called by Jesus to be "salt and light"; that is anything but a passive calling. It requires courageous action, and action, in turn, requires planning.

Your answers to the six questions will be different in many ways from any other ministry's answers, because God has created you, a unique being. Whatever your answers, wrestling with the questions wisely and well is the very foundation of master planning.

It's time to move from the realm of values and philosophy to the realm of regulations and codes—another important part of master planning! But first, let's check in with our friend Pastor Bob.

Chapter Three:

Pastor Bob's Progress

"You know, honey," Bob told his wife Karen at dinner one night, "I can't believe how far we have come in just six months. Last winter I was nearly ready to pack it in and go find something to sell or build for a living; I was really at the end of my rope. But this new project team has breathed some life back into me. I don't think we are out of the woods yet, or that we have everything figured out, but I can actually feel some hope for the first time in a while."

Karen smiled at her husband. "You know, I can really see the difference in you. Tom's friend has really helped, hasn't he?"

The morning after Bob had left the dark church parking lot in despair, Tom had called him. He gave the pastor the phone number of a friend who worked to help churches navigate the master-planning process. Reluctant at first, Bob agreed to meet with the consultant, and eventually introduced him to other senior members of the project team. Together they agreed to invite the consultant to help facilitate (Bob had never like that word, but now he was coming to understand it) their master-planning process.

To be honest, the process had moved slower than Bob had wanted. There were nights when he wanted to pound the conference room table and cry, "Let's get on with this!" The consultant was covering topics such as vision, strategy, and DNA—topics about which Bob assumed the entire leadership team had consensus. After all, the church had clear documents about such things.

However, over time, Bob discovered that just because a document has been written and approved does not mean all involved agree with it and understand it. One eye-opening discussion had come when the consultant challenged the team to talk about their "target market."

Bob was ready with an answer. "Well, we are really clear about that. We are targeting young families between the ages of thirty and forty who live within a three-mile radius of our church." Much to Bob's surprise, an older member of the team then cleared his throat and began to speak, at first hesitantly but with growing warmth.

"Pastor, I know young families are important; after all, children represent the future of our church. Still, sometimes I think we appear a bit exclusive. After all, Jesus died for *all* people. And didn't Paul say that he had become all things to all people so that some might be saved? I have some qualms about focusing on just one market, when many diverse communities out there need to know Christ!"

Bob was taken aback, but it was soon clear that others felt the same way. At first, the pastor wanted to drown out the questioning voices with logic and reason. When that proved futile, he wanted to ask if they had been paying attention when he was in the role of vision-caster. One dark night he confided in Karen that he was considering resigning because he wasn't sure that the other leaders of the church believed in his vision for ministry.

Over a period of weeks, though, the heat of the initial discussions transformed into the light of increased clarity and unity. The project team came to a new understanding of their vision and DNA as a church. After long discussions—often difficult ones—about what was a value for the church and what was non-essential, the leaders forged a real and growing consensus about the meanings of words they had used for years.

The real turning point had come the night the consultant looked around the room and addressed the leaders, speaking slowly and firmly. "I need to ask you to wrestle with a hard question. You are coming to a real clarity about your target, DNA, values, and vision. You have done great work! But now you have to stare down a scary question. What if you don't live those things out? What if you don't make the strategic adaptations and facilities decisions that will enable you to fulfill your calling? What is the cost to your church? To this community? What if you miss what God has for you?"

There was a long silence. When it passed, however, the group began a long and fruitful discussion. For the first time, the leaders were not attempting to define and clarify ideals, or to defend positions; rather, they began to take account of the cost of ministry success or failure. Suddenly, they were not a collection of representatives advocating for different philosophies and ministry areas; they were one team, fighting for a common purpose, working toward a common destiny.

Dinner ended and Bob began to clear the dishes. "You know, Karen," he mused, "there is a lot I don't understand yet about this process. There are some really baffling technical issues about zoning and requirements and variances I—that is, *we* have to grapple with. We have a long way to go. But just coming this far, I can see how we, as a church, can get to where we are going together."

He paused as he filled the dishwasher. "I like the sound of 'together.'"

Chapter Four:

From the Outside In

"I've often thought that if our zoning boards could be put in charge of botanists, of zoologists and geologists, and people who know about the earth, we would have much more wisdom in such planning than we have when we leave it up to the engineers."

—*William O. Douglas, Supreme Court Justice (1898–1980)*

M any ministry professionals will struggle with the amount of technical detail in this chapter. You have received training in teaching, leading, and caring for the souls of the people God has given you to lead, not in the more business-oriented aspects of leading a ministry. You know that your ministry's

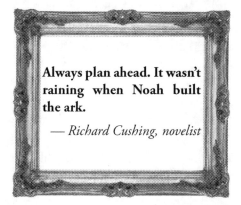

Always plan ahead. It wasn't raining when Noah built the ark.

— *Richard Cushing, novelist*

physical plant is important, but more than likely, you have neither the inclination nor the desire to master details about municipal codes, easements, equitable liens, and water retention issues.

I assure you that this is important information. Please don't skip over this material because you have a compelling vision and you assume everything else will fall into line as a result. That mindset, though understandable, is a sign of a fatal mistake: living by faith while ignoring facts (more on the faith/fact dichotomy later). In the master-planning process, both faith and facts are of crucial importance.

I have compiled a list of many of the items that you must address before any pretty pictures (concept drawings) can be developed. In most cases, your project team should be commissioned to gather this on behalf of the team and the ministry. Do not feel as if you or your leadership has to obtain this on your own.

If you are a ministry professional, your most significant contribution during this phase of the process is likely to be the choice of the right members for your team: men and women who bring expertise and experience in areas where you have not necessarily been trained. As a matter of fact, this list can actually serve as a tool as you are interviewing project team partners and considering who is best to serve with you in this venture. While our list is perhaps not comprehensive, I believe that it will prove to be a useful guide. Each of these items must be considered as you craft your master plan.

A) Phase I Environmental Study

In the real estate and development industry, this is referred to as a "look-see." According to Wikipedia (www.wikipedia.com), it is further defined as a report prepared for a real estate holding which identifies potential or existing environmental contamination liabilities. The analysis, often called an ESA, typically addresses both the underlying land as well as physical improvements to the property; however, techniques applied in a Phase I ESA never include actual collection of physical samples or chemical analyses of any kind. Scrutiny of the land includes examination of potential soil contamination, groundwater quality, surface water quality and sometimes issues related to hazardous substance uptake by biota. The examination of a site may include: definition of any chemical residues within structures; identification of possible asbestos containing building materials; inventory of hazardous substances stored or used on site; assessment of mold and mildew; and evaluation of other indoor air quality parameters.[1] Contaminated sites are often referred to as 'brownfield sites.' In severe cases, brownfield sites may be added to the National Priorities List where they will be subject to the U.S. Environmental Protection Agency's Superfund program.

Actual sampling of soil, air, groundwater, and building materials is typically not conducted during a Phase I ESA. The Phase I ESA is merely the first step in the process of environmental due diligence. If a site is considered contaminated, a Phase II Environmental Site Assessment may be conducted. This is a more detailed investigation involving chemical analysis for hazardous substances and/or petroleum hydrocarbons.

A variety of actions[2] can cause a Phase I study to be performed for a commercial property. The most common are:

- Purchase of real property by a person or entity not previously on title.
- Contemplation by a new lender to provide a loan on the subject real estate.
- Application to a public agency for change of use or other discretionary land use permit.

If the Phase I ESA indicates any potential issues, additional assessments will have to be performed.

Phase II Environmental Site Assessment: This investigation collects original samples of soil, groundwater, or building materials and analyzes them for quantitative values of various contaminants.[3] This investigation is normally undertaken when a Phase I ESA determines a likelihood of site contamination.

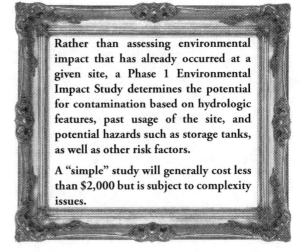

Rather than assessing environmental impact that has already occurred at a given site, a Phase 1 Environmental Impact Study determines the potential for contamination based on hydrologic features, past usage of the site, and potential hazards such as storage tanks, as well as other risk factors.

A "simple" study will generally cost less than $2,000 but is subject to complexity issues.

Phase III Environmental Site Assessment: This investigation involves remediation of a site. Phase III investigations aim to delineate the physical extent of contamination based on recommendations made in Phase II assessments. Phase III investigations may involve intensive testing, sampling, and monitoring; "fate and transport" studies and other modeling; and the design of feasibility studies for remediation and remedial plans. This study normally involves assessment of alternative cleanup methods, costs, and logistics. The study report details the steps taken to perform site cleanup and the follow-up monitoring for residual contaminants.

B) Research and Deed Restrictions

Virtually every deed for a piece of property has some restrictions or restoration covenants. A deed restriction is a legal obligation imposed on a buyer of real estate by the seller. Such restrictions frequently "run with the land" and are enforceable on subsequent buyers of the property.

Deed restrictions, also known as restrictive covenants, are commonly registered against commercial properties. General covenants, such as those restricting the heights of structures or forbidding certain "dirty" businesses (e.g., feedlots or chemical production facilities), are common in areas located near residential communities. Developers may seek to restrict the type of business allowed to operate in a certain area; a purchaser of land in a research park, for example, may not be allowed to construct a bingo parlor or a tool-and-die factory. A commercial property may also include a restrictive covenant forbidding the sale of certain items, such as pornography or liquor, on the property.

Residential covenants are relatively common with most deeds. Some residential covenants are fairly straightforward, such as those preventing owners from removing healthy trees, fundamentally altering historically important structures, or directly harming property values. Others, however, are more nuanced; some restrictive covenants may govern what color a structure's exterior is painted, what and how many exterior decorations are allowed, or where cars may be parked. In working with ministries, I have encountered restrictive covenants that limit the height of steeples, determine maximum land coverage by impervious items, or even allow or disallow the use of the property as a church or other ministry organization. As you develop your master plan and look at physical sites for your facilities, it is important to know of any restrictions and whether or not there are any "go/no go" issues that must be resolved. While many municipalities allow ministry facilities to be located within a residential zoning and classification, the deed restrictions may have conditions that would supersede the actual zoning.

C) Title Search for Easements, Reservations, Liens and other Encumbrances or Limiting Factors

The buyer of a property will usually purchase title insurance, which offers protection from any title problems that may arise after sale, such as liens that were missed during the title search. The title insurance company submits a report and issues an insurance policy in support of its findings. So what is a title search?

A title search is a process performed primarily to determine the answer to three questions:

- Can the seller legally sell all or part of the property?
- What kinds of restrictions or allowances pertain to the use of the land (real covenants, easements, or other servitudes)?
- Do any liens exist on the property that need to be addressed, such as mortgages, back taxes, mechanics' liens, or other assessments?

Anyone may do a title search and review documents concerning conveyances of land, since these documents are a matter of public record. In most cases an attorney or a title company does this kind of research, but anyone with the time to do so can gather this information. Title searches are most often carried out before contracting is completed between parties and sometimes during the escrow phase of a closing.

There are several reasons for performing a title search. One may also be carried out when an owner of a certain real property wishes to mortgage his property, and the bank requires him to insure the transaction. In the case of a ministry purchasing land, I highly recommend that this search be a contingency to any offer to purchase, and that it be performed as early in the transaction as possible. Even if you already own the property, it would be prudent to do this assessment again. You do not want to invest a great deal of time and money only to find out that there is a restriction that forbids or otherwise negatively affects the work already performed.

A title report may show any easements, meaning recorded legal rights, to the property or portions of the property. A previous owner may have legally given a neighbor the right to share the driveway, or the city may have a right to strips of the property for installing power lines, communication lines, water pipes, or sewer pipes. There may also be "reservations" granted to a utility company which give the utility the opportunity to impose the easement at a later time.

A "full coverage search" is usually done when creating a title report for sale/resale transactions and for a transaction that involves construction loans. It generally includes searches related to property liens; easements; covenants, conditions and restrictions agreements (CC&Rs); and resolutions and ordinances that will affect the real property in question.

A common issue discovered during a title search is a lien. A lien is any legal recorded claim against a property. These encumbrances are placed against real property as a "blemish" requiring payment for a claim by another party. The claim encumbers the property as a means to collect money owed, such as a mortgage, property taxes, or an unpaid debt owed to a contractor who performed work on the property. There are several types of liens you might encounter:

Equitable lien: a property is held as collateral and the parties agree in a document that the property will be used to secure the debt.

General liens: related to real estate and personal property. Court ordered judgments, probate actions, and IRS taxes fall under this category.

Judgment lien: the result of an action by a party or government agency through a court of law to collect payment on a claim.

Involuntary lien: real estate property taxes created by state statutes. These taxes are a claim against the property which the property owner assumes during purchase. Unpaid taxes can result in a specific involuntary lien.

Specific liens: special assessments and mechanics liens. Unpaid contractors from repair and remodeling projects can file a specific lien. Property associations and local governing bodies can issue special assessments for repairs and improvements. Failure to pay these special assessments can result in a lien being placed against a property.

Voluntary lien: mortgages and other voluntary agreements. For example, a mortgage holder may voluntarily agree that the mortgage lien is security for the lender in case of default on the loan.

Liens on ministry property have unique consequences. If you are looking to purchase property, then you need all the liens removed, just as if you were buying property for a house. However, some liens on your existing property, such as the specific liens, may not affect you until you try to sell the property, at which time a buyer would want them all removed. In addition, some states require that a lien be perfected, or a statement of the collateral put on file, by the party claiming it; this must be done in order to file a lawsuit against the property owner. The obvious downside of liens on your campus is that they are a matter of public record and can damage your esteem in the community. I strongly recommend that you seek legal counsel regarding any potential or current liens on your current or future real property.

D) Topography Issues

According to Dictionary.com (www.dictionary.com), *topography* is defined as:

1. The detailed mapping or charting of the features of a relatively small area, district or locality.
2. The detailed description, especially by means of surveying, of particular localities, as cities, towns, or estates.
3. The relief features or surface configurations of an area.

In laymen's terms, this is a surveying process that indicates how the land lies and describes its slopes, inclines, and reliefs. The topography of a site has enormous impact on the cost of development.

If you have a steep lot, then you need to consider a project that includes some multi-level structure. If the site is totally flat (which sites rarely are), then you must consider drainage issues. No site is void of topography issues.

Often, topography comes into play when a church feels that it has got an opportunity to purchase land for a price "too good to be true." It is not unheard of for a ministry to purchase land for up to 50 percent off of market price or appraised value and then have to spend 100 percent of the value because of challenges related to topography issues.

E) Sub-surface Investigation

Dirt is dirt, right? Not true. Not all dirt was created equally, and as such, it is prudent to do a certain level of sub-surface soil investigation. When you hear terms like *soil boring, geotechnical investigation, sampling, soil test,* and *foundation investigation,* you are in the realm of sub-surface investigation.

This investigation reveals whether or not the material under the top soil will be able to support a proposed structure. Just about any site can be built upon, so the issue is how much it will cost to provide the required bearing capacity for the proposed structure. Required remediation can either be accomplished by modifying the soil itself, or by modifying the building components. Each can be an acceptable option, with its own set of cost implications.

For example, if you have good soil conditions, you can incorporate a shallow foundation system. But what if the sub-surface soil is not as favorable? You might have to incorporate a number of remedial methodologies; such systems may include driven pilings, poured pilings, undercut and controlled fill, caissons, and helical piers. Each of these has a significant impact on the rest of the project. The earlier these issues can be determined, the better for projecting cost expectations and making structural modifications. There are very few things more discouraging than spending months planning and only then finding out your chosen site has poor soil conditions that will cost you tens or hundreds of thousands of dollars to correct.

F) Wetlands/Watershed/Flood Plain/Water Table Issues

Water is a powerful natural element; it demands your attention as well. You may already be familiar with the following terms from having discussed property purchases or development of your current property, but let's clarify exactly what each of them describes.

A *wetland* is an area of land whose soil is saturated, at least seasonally and possibly permanently, with moisture. Shallow pools of water may also partially or completely cover such areas. Generally, this "permeated land" is not suitable for development. Federal law also protects wetlands as areas with very limited development potential.

A *water table* is the level at which the groundwater pressure is equal to atmospheric pressure. It is essentially the depth at which the first water is found under the surface of the soil. That depth can directly affect development cost, particularly in coastal areas where the ground elevation is relatively close to sea level and thus limits the depth of a structure's foundation.

Watershed, also known as a drainage basin, is an area of land where rainfall or snow-melt drains downhill into a body of water, such as a river, lake, reservoir, estuary, wetland, sea, or ocean. The drainage basin includes not only the streams and rivers that convey the water, but also the land surfaces from which the water drains into those channels.

A *flood plain* is a flat, or nearly flat, area of land adjacent to a stream or river that experiences occasional or periodic flooding. It includes the floodway, which consists of the stream channel and adjacent areas that carry flood flows, and the flood fringes, which are areas covered by the flood, but which do not experience a strong current.

Each of these conditions can limit the amount of development that can be performed on a site, and each can have an impact on the cost of development. Understanding water issues is critical when purchasing land and developing both new or existing property. You may need a specialty engineer to make a final determination.

*   *   *

Let's Take a Break

The great majority of this chapter contains some pretty heady stuff, and feels a little cumbersome. So let's take a quick respite from technical terms and definitions and look at an example of what might have happened if we had had all of these regulations when Noah was building the ark.

What if Noah had to build the ark today?

And the Lord spoke to Noah and said: "In six months I'm going to make it rain until the whole earth is covered with water and all the evil people are destroyed. But I want to save a few good people, and two of every kind of living thing on the planet. I am ordering you to build me an ark." And in a flash of lightning He delivered the specifications for an ark.

"OK," said Noah, trembling in fear and fumbling with the blueprints.

"Six months, and it starts to rain," thundered the Lord. "You'd better have the ark completed, or learn how to swim for a very long time."

And six months passed. The skies began to cloud up and rain began to fall. The Lord saw that Noah was sitting in his front yard, weeping. And there was no ark.

"Noah," shouted the Lord, "where is my ark?"

A lightning bolt crashed into the ground next to Noah. "Lord, please forgive me!" begged Noah. "I did my best. But there were big problems. First I had to get a building permit for the ark construction project, and your plans didn't meet code. So I had to hire an engineer to redraw the plans. Then I got into a big fight over whether or not the ark needed a fire sprinkler system. My neighbors objected claiming I was violating zoning by building the ark in my front yard, so I had to get a variance from the city planning commission.

"Then I had a big problem getting enough wood for the ark because there was a ban on cutting trees to save the Spotted Owl. I had to convince U.S. Fish and Wildlife that I needed the wood to save the owls. But they wouldn't let me catch any owls. So no owls. Then the carpenters formed a union and went out on strike. I had to negotiate a settlement with the National Labor Relations Board before anyone would pick up a saw or a hammer. Now we have sixteen carpenters going on the boat, and still no owls.

"Then I started gathering up animals, and got sued by an animal rights group. They objected to me taking only two of each kind. Just when I got the suit dismissed, EPA notified me that I couldn't complete the ark without filing an environmental impact statement on your proposed flood. They didn't take kindly to the idea that they had no jurisdiction over the conduct of a Supreme Being.

"Then the Army Corps of Engineers wanted a map of the proposed new flood plan. I sent them a globe. Right now I'm still trying to resolve a complaint from the Equal Employment Opportunity Commission over how many Croatians I'm supposed to hire, the IRS has seized all my assets claiming I'm trying to avoid paying taxes by leaving the country, and I just got a notice from the state about owing some kind of use tax. I really don't think I can finish your ark for at least another five years," Noah wailed.

The sky began to clear. The sun began to shine. A rainbow arched across the sky. Noah looked up and smiled. "You mean you're not going to destroy the earth?" Noah asked, hopefully.

"Wrong!" thundered the Lord. "But being Lord of the Universe has its advantages. I fully intend to smite the Earth, but with something far worse than a flood. Something man invented himself—GOVERNMENT![4]

* * *

G) Setbacks and Right-of-Ways

In land use, a **setback** is the distance that a building or other structure is removed from a street or road, another property, a river or other stream, a shore or flood plain, or any other place that needs protection. Setbacks are generally set by municipal ordinances and can be found by doing research with the local zoning office or building official. (One side note: if the details of roadway setbacks are not incorporated in the zoning ordinances, you may have to contact the Department of Transportation for clarification.)

A **right-of-way** describes the right of a non-owning party or the public at large to traverse a piece of land. The term also

refers to the land subject to such a right. Generally, there is a predetermined manner or route of travel over the land. An easement is an example of a right-of-way. A public right-of-way permits public travel, such as a street, road, sidewalk, or footpath. Sometimes, a right-of-way may refer to a utility easement, such as a power line.

These restrictions will affect the amount of land usable for development. In most cases you cannot build, park on, or otherwise develop within these areas. In fact, in many municipalities, you will have a yard or street setback accompanied by a buffer zone, which, in essence, means you have two setback areas limiting the development area.

H) Tree and Landscape Issues

"What do you mean we can't cut down our trees?" That's right. In most municipalities you cannot cut down trees or clear the land without a land disturbance permit. In fact, in some areas, you cannot cut down "landmark" or "heritage" trees at all; at the very least, you cannot remove them without a public hearing and formal approval. Some areas may have a recompense process, which means that you must replace every tree removed with another tree of a designated species and of a specific diameter (typically determined by caliper inch), while others impose a fee for each tree that is removed. All of these issues will affect your development process and costs. I recommended that you obtain a tree survey at the same time that you obtain the boundary and topography survey. A tree survey will identify the location, size, and species of all of your site's trees that measure above a specified minimum diameter.

Landscaping also has a significant impact on most projects. Virtually every municipality has some level of requirement for landscaping. Landscape buffers are very common and affect not only the developable area but also the cost to the project. Have your team research and understand the zoning ordinances for landscape buffers, entrance ways, right-of way landscape requirements, roadway landscaping, and any other requirements they might find on the books.

Many zoning ordinances will have buffer exceptions that allow a hybrid approach to the landscape buffer through some combination of fencing and denser landscape material. You may want to exceed the minimum requirements, however, merely for the benefit of the aesthetics of the campus. The appearance of your campus makes the first impression on the community and your guests, and that first impression will shape their perception of the kind of ministry and neighbor you are and will be in the future.

I) Building Codes, Accessibility Codes, Fire Protection, and More

There are many different groups and people who will serve as the *authority having jurisdiction* (AHJ) over any land or building development or expansion. Some are state regulated, while others are governed by a county, city, township, province, or municipality. There are also some codes and governing bodies that have national acceptance which is then interpreted and enforced on a local or state level. The International Code Council attempted to unify building codes when they developed the International Building Code (IBC).

The International Building Code (www.iccsafe.org)

However, many states have adopted only some portions of the IBC. Others have customized the IBC by adding amendments. To further complicate the situation, not every state or municipality uses the same edition of the IBC. Some use IBC 2000, others IBC 2003, others IBC 2006. As you can imagine, this often creates immense confusion!

Here's an example of how the same code (IBC) has been modified in the adjacent states of North and South Carolina. The IBC, in its native form, requires that you provide an automatic fire sprinkler system for any "assembly occupancy" (which describes a worship space, fellowship space, or even a multipurpose space) that can accommodate three hundred people or more. There are two ways to determine occupancy. If you have fixed seating (seats that are bolted or otherwise attached to the floor), you can use a measurement of

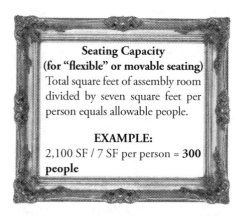

Seating Capacity
(for "flexible" or movable seating)
Total square feet of assembly room divided by seven square feet per person equals allowable people.

EXAMPLE:
2,100 SF / 7 SF per person = **300 people**

eighteen inches per seat. This eighteen-inch rule applies to pews and other forms of bench seating. But if you are going to utilize moveable seating (stacked or folding chairs), then occupancy is calculated by determining the square footage of the assembly space and dividing it by seven square feet per person.

Therefore, if you have an assembly space that is 2,100 square feet or larger, and you intend to use flexible seating, you must have a fire sprinkler. The state of South Carolina holds to this interpretation of the code very tightly: if you are a church in South Carolina and you intend to build any space that could be deemed an assembly occupancy with flexible seating, then any room over 2,100 square feet will need to be equipped with an automatic sprinkler system.

Tough requirement, right? That's what South Carolina's neighbor state thought. So North Carolina added amendments to the IBC. In North Carolina, it is only necessary to install a fire sprinkler system in a room of 12,000 square feet if it is being used for a place of worship. If you are in North Carolina and want to build an assembly-occupancy facility with flexible seating, you can build a room that can accommodate 1,000 people before you are required to install sprinklers. This results in a huge difference in factors that churches in North and South Carolina must consider.

Know which code applies to your ministry. Understand how it affects your project. And have your team conduct a detailed code analysis as you get started.

J) DOT Issues

The DOT (Department of Transportation) can influence your master plan and project development in many ways. The following is a partial list of items you will need to take into consideration.

1. **Curb Cuts**. Can you add a driveway from your site to the adjoining road(s)? If so, how many and how far apart must they be?

2. **Traffic Counts.** Many metropolitan areas require that you retain a firm to perform a traffic impact study to include traffic counts. This data, in concert with the municipalities' projection of the number of vehicles that your developed property will add to the traffic count, determines the total projected traffic on those roadways. Many of these major roadways have designated "trip counts," codifying how many cars per day can have access to the roadway. If the projected count of new vehicles plus the existing traffic count exceeds the total trip counts, your project could be in jeopardy. I have been involved with some projects where the DOT or local municipality required the church to buy additional trip counts, which is essentially a DOT "tax" on organizations that helps to pay for road improvements.

3. **Acceleration and Deceleration Lanes**. The municipality or DOT may mandate acceleration and/or deceleration lanes to provide for the safe access to the developed property. They may also require special signage or traffic signals. Factors such as the number of lanes, the speed limit, and the traffic impact play a role in to all of these decisions.

K) Site Utility Availability

Site utilities have always been an issue for any development or expansion project, but with the adoption of the IBC, it becomes even more critical to consider them. One of the most noteworthy changes that the IBC brought was the requirement of fire sprinkler systems in buildings coded for an assembly occupancy.

At first, this may not seem like a big deal. You'll just install a sprinkler system if you need to, right? Sure ... as long as you have a water supply.

Do you have public water available? If so, does it have ample pressure to fight a fire? There are several alternate methods to provide the water supply, but none of them is economical. Water towers, water tanks, and monitored ponds are all usable options, if your local fire marshal agrees, but each is a very expensive proposition. I have built ponds to accommodate sprinkler requirements that cost the project close to $250,000 extra—a huge chunk of money to spend for a trustworthy system you pray you will never need to utilize.

Let's talk about it in ministry terms. If you did not have to build that kind of water supply, how much more ministry space could you build? If we assume that you could build added space for $150 per square foot, then you could build another 1,700 square feet. If you are considering worship space, this equates to another one hundred

Planning is bringing the future into the present so that you can do something about it now.

— *Alan Lakein, writer*

seats or more. I trust that you are beginning to see that seemingly "technical" issues can have real Kingdom implications!

Other utilities you need to consider include the public sewer, electric service, and gas lines. Your project team should contact the local utilities early in the planning process to make sure they understand all the requirements and implications of these areas.

L) Local Review Board

In addition to written codes, many municipalities have local review boards, Development Review committees, Architectural Review Boards, and the like. I have found that coastal areas (like those in Florida and California) and resort areas are the most likely to have such public review processes. If you went to develop a property in Miami, you might have to spend between one and three years in the Development Review Committee (DRC) process *before* you can even submit for a building permit. I am seeing this level of scrutiny becoming more and more commonplace across the country.

It behooves you to find out as far in advance as possible if you will have to undergo a review, so that you can address the requisite processes and requirements. Your project team should do the due diligence to determine what other groups and organizations have influence on your project. They will need to obtain and note the dates when the groups meet so they can ensure they follow the process for submitting documents in a timely fashion. It is not uncommon for these public groups, generally comprising volunteers from the community, to meet only once a month. In order to afford themselves enough time to review the relevant documentation, they generally require you to submit your application package to them the month prior to the meeting at which you desire to be on the docket.

Remember, too, that even if you follow all the rules and regulations, your project may not be approved. What if it does not pass the first time? Don't panic; you can resubmit. Of course, the same timing holds for resubmission of your application package; as a result, you could be adding in months you did not originally budget just to get the approval you need to move ahead. The clock is ticking, and if you have not planned accordingly for this part of the process, you could be delaying the project, which may in turn affect the interest rate on your loan and the cost of materials and labor.

M) Variances and Special Use Permits

A variance is an official permit to do something forbidden by regulations, especially by building in a way or for a purpose normally forbidden by a zoning law or building code. For example, imagine a zoning ordinance that limits the height of a building to thirty feet above grade, but you have designed a building that is thirty-two feet tall. You can petition a variance for the additional two feet. Perhaps the zoning ordinance requires two hundred paved parking spaces for your project, but you do not have enough land to provide all of those spaces. You can petition a variance either to reduce the parking requirements or to allow for a certain amount of parking spaces to be located off-site.

The most common variance requests are associated with parking, building height, or setbacks. The ease of getting approval from the local authority having jurisdiction, however, is as varied as the numbers of municipalities in the country. Therefore, it pays to do some due diligence before you start this process.

A **special use permit** allows a specific exception

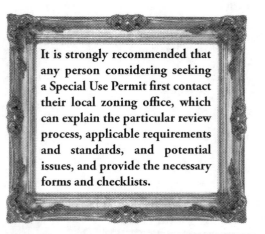

It is strongly recommended that any person considering seeking a Special Use Permit first contact their local zoning office, which can explain the particular review process, applicable requirements and standards, and potential issues, and provide the necessary forms and checklists.

to the zoning regulations. The exception must come from a list of acceptable exceptions for a particular parcel of land in a district of a particular zoning character. The local zoning authority reviews and grants special use permits.

Land use is governed by a set of regulations generally known as ordinances or municipal codes, which are authorized by the state's zoning enabling law. Within an ordinance is a list of land-use designations, commonly known as *zoning*. Each different type of zone has its own set of allowed, or *by-right* uses, and extra, or special uses that require obtaining a special use permit before building. Many times, a church will want to build in a residential area not zoned for church facilities. In order to move forward even a step, a special use permit is required.

Acquiring a special use permit represents yet another extra step that you may have to take to receive approval to build. Usually a planning commission or other legislative body must hold a public hearing in order to grant special use permits. This can introduce an unfortunate element of politics to the decision-making process, which may negatively affect your project.

N) Water Detention and Retention Issues

Most jurisdictions require that a developed parcel of land does not produce any more storm water run-off than it would have if it were undeveloped. At some point in your design process you will need to engage a civil engineer to perform a hydrology study (the study of the movement, distribution, and quality of water). While you do not need the hydrology study in the earliest phases of your process, you do need to recognize that detention and retention will need to be addressed on your site and in your master plan.

Water detention can be addressed in several ways. The development of out-fill ditches, swales, and other natural elements have the least impact on the site by taking advantage of its natural features, and are thus usually the least costly. Other means to retain and detain storm water include detention ponds, storm drainage systems, and underground retention systems.

More and more jurisdictions are becoming sensitive to storm water run-off, which makes this issue significant in your planning. If it is not an option to make use of swales, out-fill ditches, or other natural aspects of the property, then detention ponds are generally the most cost-effective, particularly if your topography will allow for gravity to bring about "sheet flowing" of the storm water to the pond. If that is not the case, then you may be able to install a system of pipes to accomplish the same net result, but at a higher development cost.

Many municipalities also have storm-water systems that are placed under public streets and right-of-ways. If such systems are available, you should explore the possibility of utilizing these resources.

O) Parking Issues—Ratios, Pervious vs. Impervious, and More

Parking lots and vehicular access on your site will most likely consume the largest physical area of any part of your project. On average, you can obtain ninety to a hundred parking spaces per acre of usable land, assuming the land is relatively level.

Virtually every municipality has a zoning ordinance that includes a section concerning parking requirements. Generally for a church, ministry facility, or assembly space, the ratios are based on a certain number of seats in your largest assembly space for every parking space. I have seen these ratios range from three to five seats per parking space.

Given that the total number of seats is calculated based on the type of seating you select, I recommend that you do your own parking count to establish your own real-world ratio over three to four weeks. Have a designated person count the number of cars you have on- and off-site during your worship service. From this data you will be able to determine your own parking ratio. I have found that most ministries need one space for every two to two-and-a-half seats. This can fall below a 2:1 ratio if you have a lot of families with teenagers or have multiple services.

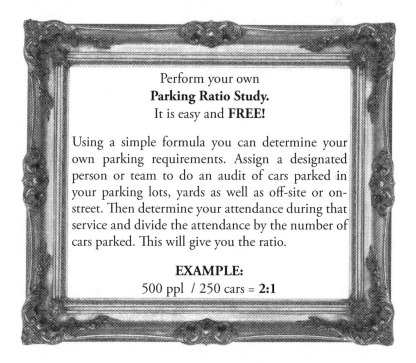

Perform your own
Parking Ratio Study.
It is easy and **FREE!**

Using a simple formula you can determine your own parking requirements. Assign a designated person or team to do an audit of cars parked in your parking lots, yards as well as off-site or on-street. Then determine your attendance during that service and divide the attendance by the number of cars parked. This will give you the ratio.

EXAMPLE:
500 ppl / 250 cars = **2:1**

Let's see how this might play out. Take our earlier example of the church with three hundred seats. Let's assume the local code has a three-to-one ratio (three seats per parking space). In this scenario you would need one hundred parking spaces (three hundred seats divided by three seats per space). That translated to between one and 1.5 acres just for parking to meet "code minimum."

That's all well and good, but what if your specific ministry needs a 2:1 ratio? In that case you need 150 spaces (three hundred seats at a 2:1 ratio). This means you will need between 1.5 and 1.75 acres just for parking. As you can see, the available land can be chewed up quickly. If you consider that the building in this scenario could be 10,000 and 15,000 square feet (or up to a third of an acre) you will need over two acres of usable and developable land just for your building and parking. Then you need to add land for the setbacks, buffers, detention and retention, green areas, and growth potential. Most churches underestimate the amount of total land they will need.

In addition to the land mass of the parking areas, you must consider what materials will these areas comprise. The most common is asphalt (black top) and most metropolitan jurisdictions require this as well. However, asphalt is an impervious material, meaning water will not pass through it. The more impervious material you have, the larger your detention and retention areas must be. Deciding on the surface covering of your parking areas early in the process will help the team determine the potential size of your detention area.

If you are in an area that allows for pervious parking surfaces, such as gravel or grass, you may want to consider these options; they can reduce the initial cost of your parking area as well as reduce the impact of impervious parking. I have worked in coastal regions that actually prefer pervious parking in order to lessen the impacts of storm water runoff.

* * *

This chapter has been full of technical detail, hasn't it? I trust you are not overwhelmed or discouraged. But if you are, let me remind you that if you are the key ministry leader, your job is not to master every technical detail, but rather to gather just the right team of people who have the expertise needed, charge them up with Kingdom vision and personal concern and support, and let them serve and lead!

Chapter Five:

Framing It Up

"Plans are worthless. Planning is essential."

— President Dwight D. Eisenhower

"By failing to prepare, you prepare to fail."

— Benjamin Franklin

At this point in the master-planning process, you have a lot of data at your disposal. It's time to move to the next step: carefully analyzing the data so that you can put the right frame in place for the ministry picture you are creating.

Before the pretty picture of your Kingdom vision can be put in the frame, you'll need to go through four areas of analysis:

1) Site Feasibility
2) Financial Evaluation
3) Space Allocation and Program Study
4) Facility Audit (for churches with existing structures)

Each of these areas of analysis will have a significant impact on your master plan.

1) Site Feasibility

You have just collected a *ton* of data related to your site. You and your project team know which codes apply, what your soil conditions are, and whether or not you have wetlands to navigate. Now, what do you do with all of this data?

The team needs to develop a project site analysis report that will focus on the following criteria:

A) How much usable land mass is available for our project? Once all of the setbacks, buffers, easements, right-of-ways, and so on have been identified, what is left? How much can be developed?

B) What are the parking criteria and how much land mass will that require? (Remember to explore not only what the jurisdiction will require, but also what your specific ministry will demand.)

C) What topography issues do we face, and how do they change the usable land mass and the placement of structures? Do we need to consider a basement or multistory structure? Do we need to address tiered parking?

D) What zoning and public/private issues need to be addressed? What are the timelines and deliverables for each? Can we build what we want with the current zoning, or do we need to obtain a special use permit? If so, how long will that take, and how far into the process can we get before it becomes a "go/no-go" issue?

E) Will any variances be required for the plan? Are there any issues that could affect the height, parking, or other parameters of our building project?

F) What utilities are available? How will their availability (or lack thereof) change the land mass? Is water and sewer available to our site, and are they of adequate size?

G) Do we have any deed or title issues to be addressed or avoided? If so, are any of them deal-breakers?

H) Are there any other reports or tests that need to be performed on the site? Will the bank require a Phase I ESA?

With this list and the subsequent analysis in hand, you will have a good understanding from which to understand the physical constraints of the property. This baseline will help the project team make recommendations in light of the physical attributes of your property, uncover any issues those attributes create, and choose next steps.

2) Financial Evaluation

Financial evaluation is a critical, albeit often-overlooked, part of the master planning process. Because they hold such a strong belief in the power of their vision, ministry leaders often assume that once that vision is communicated, the financial resources will automatically follow. Alas; this is no wiser than leaving for our family vacation without enough cash on hand to provide lodging, gas, and food.

Because most churches plan on incorporating the earliest phases of their master plan in the very near future, financial analysis must be taken into consideration and is, in fact, one of the key drivers of the process.

In more than twenty-three years of helping ministries to develop their properties, I have yet to work with any church or ministry organization that did not need money to build. They either needed cash to build their ministry tools or needed to borrow some or all of the needed funds. I have yet to find a builder who was willing to exchange manna for building materials. Because of this, I have found it extraordinarily helpful to talk about the distinction between *fact* and *faith*.

Fact or Faith?

"The bank has told us that we can borrow whatever we need." Those words may not mean exactly what they seem to; the reality is that the bank means that you can borrow whatever you need as long as it is within your payback capability, which takes into account the value of your property and its future improvements as well as your assets. Hence, you need to make sure you have adequately determined your budget of the project. In almost every case, churches are faced with a decision between fact and faith.

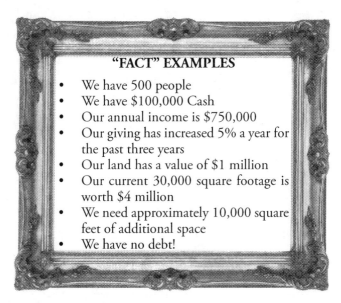

"FACT" EXAMPLES

- We have 500 people
- We have $100,000 Cash
- Our annual income is $750,000
- Our giving has increased 5% a year for the past three years
- Our land has a value of $1 million
- Our current 30,000 square footage is worth $4 million
- We need approximately 10,000 square feet of additional space
- We have no debt!

Fact, in this case, is simply what we know we can afford today. We count the liquid funds on hand and the income from tithes and offerings. We can run some projections based on the number of people in attendance and the average increase (or decrease) in our giving over the past three years. We also have other assets—our current land and physical plant. Then we have our liabilities: how much debt we currently carry, and how much space we will need and its projected cost. Those are some of the constants, the facts that a bank would look at in determining whether they would lend money to your church for a capital improvement to the property.

The *faith* definition is a bit more ambiguous. It takes into account unknowns that we trust the Lord will provide for us, such as the potential commitments in a capital stewardship campaign, the desire to sell a piece of property that the church owns, the possibility of a large single-donor contribution, or some other source outside of regular tithes and offerings. What is taken on faith has a tendency to vary with each ministry, and can have a great influence on how a project is designed or enacted. If a church believes that they can run a capital campaign and generate four times the church's annual income, and they are willing to borrow 100% against those funds, that would indicate a very high faith threshold. On the other hand, if a church does not plan on doing a capital campaign despite having no other means by which to gather resources, then that would be a very low faith threshold. Every church needs to examine itself to determine its comfort level between faith and fact, and the project needs to be designed with that level of comfort in mind.

I strongly recommend that every church plan their project with some level of faith in mind. God honors our expressions of faith in him. At the same time, if the church's comfort level falls at an extremely high level of faith, it should also make the prudent choice of creating a backup plan. A great method for this is dividing the project into multiple phases so that if, for some reason, the funds do not come through, the project need not be shelved. Too many churches have planned based on a very high faith line, have spent tens of thousands of dollars on drawings that were based on dreams and faith assumptions, and have come up short. This type of poor planning can demoralize a church and congregation and weaken its leadership.

There has been an old rule of thumb that a church can borrow three times its annual income. While that is a good starting point for preliminary budgeting, it is not enough to determine definitively what the church can afford. Three times the annual income of a church that is already spending its entire budget is a meaningless number, because there is no margin of error for additional payments or expenditures. In the same way, a church with a large debt load cannot count on the "three times" rule.

A slightly more realistic, but similar, rule is that a church can afford to borrow three times its annual income, less debt, plus cash. This rule is still not perfectly reliable, as current budget spending versus current giving and income calculations may skew the equation.

So, what *is* a good rule of thumb that represents a responsible balance between fact and faith?

I believe that every church should consider regular capital stewardship campaigns. Such campaigns not only raise money for a specific project, but also tend to grow the faith and generosity of members; they also provide leadership a perfect opportunity to communicate the principles of biblical stewardship. A capital stewardship campaign that could raise 1.7 times a church's annual income is a responsible, conservative, very reachable goal. This is far less than most stewardship campaigns would indicate but is a number that I have found to be a good conservative average during my years of work with churches. This number assumes you engage a professional stewardship consulting firm, as the average for an "in-house" campaign is closer to only 1 times a church's annual income.

If you assume that 1.7 times your income is a reasonable goal, I encourage you to assume that you will actually collect 75 to 80 percent of the amount pledged. There are a number of reasons:

a) Some people relocate, so they no longer give to the church they once attended;

b) Some people will lose jobs, be displaced, or otherwise have to change occupations, which causes financial challenges;

c) Lifestyle changes have an impact on giving: kids go to college; someone is in an accident; an elderly parent requires care.

Given these factors, let's use an 80-percent collectible estimate for discussion purposes. Let's also assume that this 80 percent will be collected over a three-year period. Now take the 80 percent and divide it by thirty-six months to establish the amount of "income" that a bank might use when considering a church's financial assets (over and above the operating budget). This "cushion" is necessary collateral; it can be used for any possible debt services during the project.

It is important here to note the difference between debt service and debt retirement. In most cases, churches utilize a capital campaign to do one of two things: generate an infusion of cash as a sort of "first fruits" of a longer campaign, or to build a reserve for debt servicing.

A ministry's first campaign is generally used for debt servicing, while subsequent campaigns are then required for debt retirement. Make sure that your congregation is clear on this point. If your desire is to use the capital campaign funds either to retire your debt or to pay in cash for the project, then you will need to postpone the project until all of the monies have been collected. While I have seen this work in a very few instances, there are significant challenges. First, you would need to consider the cost of inflation. If you intend to build a three-million-dollar project and you have commitments for all three million dollars (based on 80 percent collected), but you intend to wait for the entire amount to be collected over three years of your campaign, you are going to wind up short in three years. If construction inflation were to increase at a rate of 5 percent per year, you could be looking at an additional $450,000 that you would need to raise just to keep up with inflation.

Another issue is the loss of momentum. It has been my experience that people give to see something happen, and when it is delayed, they lose motivation to continue giving. The momentum of, and enthusiasm for, the project dries up (or slows to a trickle) until they see some dirt moving or other activity on the site.

Finally, consider the opportunity loss of the ministry: If your ministry has reached a point of facility saturation—which may be why you are considering an expansion program in the first place—consider the opportunities lost by not providing the facilities to accomplish ministry. If you wait three years to have all the cash in hand before you start to build, you could be four or more years away from being able to utilize the facility. At that point, will you still need the facility? Will the people you had hoped to serve have found another place to meet their needs?

Let's take our ratio and run the numbers out for a case study. Assume a church with an annual budget of $500,000. Given our ratio, we could estimate total commitments of $850,000. Eighty percent of that total number is $680,000, so we can assume that that is the amount we have to use during the capital campaign, at the "burn rate"/expenditure of $18,889 per month. That amount of money, at an interest rate of 7 percent amortized over twenty-five years, would allow the church to debt service a loan in the amount of approximately $2,675,000.

Now you see how the numbers work

> **Danger, Danger, Will Robinson!** This calculation has a potential downside that you must evaluate before you engage in this methodology. It assumes that after three years your general giving will have increased to match or exceed what the campaign generated **OR** you must do subsequent campaigns.

and what sort of contribution levels you can expect using the fact and faith continuum. What's next?

The next step is to determine your *total project budget*. This is a term that is confused with a similar term, *building budget*. What is the difference?

The building budget is just that—the budget to build the structures from the footings up. On the other hand, the total project budget includes the projected cost for *every aspect* of the project, including the building of the structures. What are these aspects, in addition to actual construction costs? The following is a representative list of such items.

Total Project Budget Items

1) Civil engineering and other survey and geotechnical services
2) Architecture and engineering fees
3) Permit costs
4) Property insurance (commonly referred to as builder's risk insurance)
5) Legal assistance
6) Specialty engineering services (landscape architect, audio/visual, lighting, commercial kitchen, etc.)
7) Acoustical design
8) Interior design
9) Thematic design and implementation
10) Furniture, fixtures and equipment
11) Cost of AVL systems
12) Technology/IT design and implementation
13) Capital Stewardship Campaign costs, including multi-media
14) Demolition/renovation cost (if applicable)
15) Inflationary contingency
16) Design and construction contingency
17) Financing cost (loan fees, title insurance, points, etc.)
18) Permit expediting services, if required
19) Site work, grading, utilities, paving, etc.
20) Landscaping
21) Construction Management (if appropriate)

I advise clients that they can expect that these items will require 40 to 45 percent of the total project budget. This means that a church would only have 55 to 60 percent, give or take for the actual construction costs. So when I hear a ministry leader say, "We want to build a three-million-dollar project," I always ask if they mean a three million building budget or total project budget. If it is the latter, that would

Plans fail for lack of counsel, but with many advisers they succeed.

— Proverbs 15:22

lead me to believe that they will have $1.65–1.8 million to spend on the actual building. Too many ministries don't understand this difference and suffer a nasty shock a few steps into the process. I don't want that to happen to you!

3) Space Allocation and Program Study

This next step is a combination of two processes: space allocation of existing structures (if any), and programmatic study of designed and needed space.

If your ministry has existing structures that you intend to continue to use, then you will need to conduct a space allocation study. It is important to do a room-by-room evaluation of all your space to determine the following:

1) Size of the room
2) Current use and by what groups
3) What days the space is used
4) How many are in attendance at each use
5) Are there any untouchable "sacred cows"?
6) How many times the room "turns" in a week or a day (set up, tear down, re-set up)

This step clarifies whether or not your existing space is being used in the most effective way. More than once, I have seen this step result in a church determining that it needs to build less new space and hence spend less money! The primary design tool in master planning is the Program Study, and it involves several steps. The first step is "discovery," which is often the first time that ministry leaders get down to nuts and bolts about daily ministry realities.

For example, we might consider the children of our ministry. How many kids are in the nursery now? What is our ratio of children to adults? Do we expect that to change as the ministry grows? Those are just a few, and just related to the children's needs; the leadership must take a clear-eyed, honest look at dozens of questions just like these.

This discovery process can include as many leaders as you deem appropriate; the most important thing is to have a good cross-section. If the people involved in this process are all involved in the worship ministry, you would find that their priorities would revolve around the size of the platform, the acoustics, the amount of lighting, the greenroom space, and so on. They may not understand the details pertinent to the children's space or to the gathering area.

After discovery, you must hold a debriefing with the ministry's senior leadership. This will allow the senior leadership to hear directly from those involved in discovery, as well as to ensure that the desires and needs of the individual ministry leaders are in tune with the overall vision of the church as a whole. If you find that your individual leaders are getting off base or chasing endeavors inconsistent with the vision, you must work to achieve unity of purpose before you get much farther down the road in the master planning process.

Now, it is time to add a narrative element to your study, bringing facts together with dreams. If we plan for X kids in the nursery, then at Y square feet per child, we will need Z square feet. In

Children Space Planning Example
CLASSROOM:
40 children (toddlers) @ 35 SF/child =1,400 SF
TOILET ROOM:
Minimum of 25 SF
STORAGE CLOSET:
Suggested size of 25 SF
TOTAL: **1,450 SF**

addition, we want a private toilet room for each classroom and do not want more than W kids per teacher and assistant. We also want lockable storage closets and shelving in each room.

This process should be completed for every ministry area. At the completion of these discussions, you should have a net usable square footage number. Then you need to account for common areas, typically restrooms, corridors, an electrical room, a sprinkler room, mechanical room(s), storage areas, and wall thickness. These items will add a grossing factor that can easily increase the building size fifteen to twenty-five percent over the net usable square feet.

For example, your team may have determined that you need 20,000 square feet of usable square footage. We now need to accommodate the ancillary spaces mentioned above. If we assume that you need a grossing factor of 20 percent, this will increase your total square footage needs to 24,000 square feet. When determining gross square footage (which is the most common measurement when discussing the total square footage of a building), remember to measure from the outside faces of the building. Any other methodology for measuring will give you a false sense of the actual size of the overall structure.

4) Facility Audit

This step will help you determine if your existing physical structures are compatible with your long range plan or if you will need to make radical changes to your current infrastructure.

I recommend conducting a two-part evaluation, involving both a physical and a functional analysis.

The physical analysis addresses all the elements of the primary structural system (what holds the building up and together), the secondary structural elements (what you see and what keeps the weather out), the service systems, (mechanical, electrical and plumbing), and the safety standards.

- Is the structure generally sound?
- Are the heating and ventilation systems adequate?
- What is the condition of the wiring? The plumbing?
- Are the floors solid and level? Will they hold their intended weight loads?
- What is the practical, useful life expectancy of the facility?
- How much are owning and operating costs?
- Are there preventive maintenance schedules and related budget resources in place?
- If significant buildings and grounds investments are required, what are the economics of the situation?
- Is the roof in good condition? Does it drain well?
- Does the structure meet building codes? Is it worth keeping? Can it be renovated/modified? Should it be?

The functional analysis evaluates how well the building fulfills its current intended purpose, and how it will fulfill its purpose in the long term. It also determines how accessible the building is for those with various handicaps, especially those prevalent among an aging population.

- Are users of the facility crowded, or is there wasted space? What is the ratio of non-usable to usable space?
- Does the facility have historical significance? Is it significant in terms of your heritage? Would it have value to someone else?
- Is the property conveniently located for other development?
- Does the facility meet your program needs?
- Does the building offer operational efficiencies? Could it?
- Does the facility "fit" in the context of the overall property?
- Is this the highest and best use of the site and facilities?
- Do adjacent spaces make sense? Can this be changed?
- Are there challenges with the Americans with Disability Act and access issues?
- Will it/can it meet compliance for standards—codes, licensing, etc.?
- Does the facility deliver your image and positioning in the market and to your target?
- Does the facility support your mission/purpose/vision?

With all this analysis complete, the moment of reckoning is upon us. Does the financial analysis reconcile with the functional analysis?

What do you do if your financial spreadsheet indicates you can afford 20,000 square feet but your program study says you desire 50,000 square feet? This is where the leadership must meet its highest challenge, as you must negotiate among those passionately committed—and rightfully so—to their own ministry areas. Every ministry leader believes that he or she must have all of the space indicated on the program study. No one can give up an inch.

How do you move ahead? I suggest three steps. First, remind all leaders of the mission, vision, target, and DNA of your church to ensure that everyone is in lockstep agreement, not just intellectually, but with heart and soul. Next, review your facts and your faith; you made some key, shaping decisions during the process of understanding that dynamic tension. Finally, resist the urge to talk about "cutting" ministries or plans. It is much more helpful to talk of intentionally phasing certain aspects in over the course of the project, as time and finances permit.

These discussions will be challenging, perhaps even emotional. But in the strongest possible terms I urge you to have them at this point in the process. The short-term pain may well result in increased clarity and unity. In any event, you will avoid the long-term pain of demoralized leaders and financial peril.

Chapter Six:

Filling in the Frame

"You see things and say 'Why?' But I dream things that never were; and I say 'Why not?'"

— George Bernard Shaw

We began by talking about how every ministry leader wants "pretty pictures," a visual embodiment of a compelling ministry dream. The intention of my work here has been to convince you that the pretty pictures will be more realistic and will have a much better chance of coming to life if you are willing to take the leadership challenge of engaging in a thorough, intelligent,

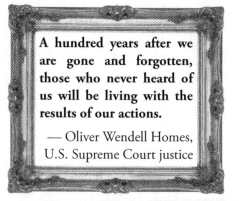

A hundred years after we are gone and forgotten, those who never heard of us will be living with the results of our actions.

— Oliver Wendell Homes, U.S. Supreme Court justice

honest master-planning process. But there comes a time for pictures—and it is now!

The drawings phase of master planning is both exciting and revealing. A lot of things will become evident to you and the project team once you have drawings in front of you.

Is there adequate usable land for all of the desired building footprints, parking, buffers, vehicular aisles, storm water detention, athletic fields, and septic fields? If so, then praise the Lord! If not, then what? Can we buy more land? Can we modify our buildings to reduce the footprints by going vertical with multiple-story buildings? Should we relocate? Should we adjust our ministry programs to consider multiple services? You will find there are many challenges and questions to tackle!

You will also see if there will be any major issues with the topography that will either drive up the cost of the project or require an adjustment of the building structures or placement. Do we need to add retaining walls? Will the storm water flow properly? Will a basement make good sense? Will the site need significant cut or fill? Will the sewage makes use of gravity to flow? Will parking have to be tiered?

In addition to the insight it offers concerning site conditions, the drawings phase of the master plan is a tremendous tool for communicating vision. After all, isn't that why you wanted it in the first place? The physical manifestation of the master plan will allow the church body to understand the direction the ministry leadership believes God is leading by actually seeing the vision.

At this point you will have most of the data needed to make an informed decision about the next steps to take, including whether the best next step is a pause. There is no shame in stepping back and slowing the process; if you are not ready, the worst thing you can do is lead the church in to an ill-advised project. At the same time, it can be almost as damaging to fail to proceed if you truly believe that the Lord is leading your ministry to reach your target and fulfill your passions. Don't squander this opportunity to further the work of the gospel.

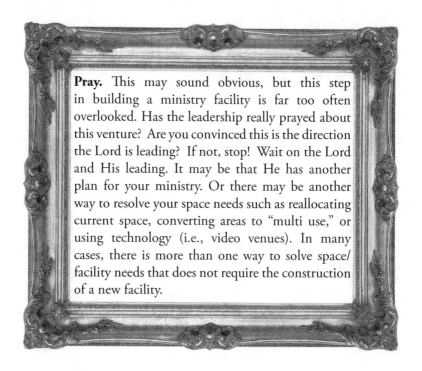

Pray. This may sound obvious, but this step in building a ministry facility is far too often overlooked. Has the leadership really prayed about this venture? Are you convinced this is the direction the Lord is leading? If not, stop! Wait on the Lord and His leading. It may be that He has another plan for your ministry. Or there may be another way to resolve your space needs such as reallocating current space, converting areas to "multi use," or using technology (i.e., video venues). In many cases, there is more than one way to solve space/facility needs that does not require the construction of a new facility.

One last piece of encouragement for you as you reach the end of your project: resist the temptation to believe that now the master planning process is done. Don't believe that all of your work is now useless, is merely gathering dust in a binder on a forgotten corner of your bookshelf.

A master plan is not a one-and-done document. It is a living organism that should be reviewed on a regular basis. Depending on the growth of your church and other external factors, you may want to review the master plan every couple of years. Things change, people change; communities change; methodologies change; society itself changes. All of this can affect the master plan and it may well need revising along the way.

As you move forward with the master plan, let me encourage you to follow these simple steps:

1. Pray continuously
2. Dream
3. Plan thoroughly
4. Maintain realism
5. Draw pretty pictures!
6. Express your vision
7. Repeat

You have done lots of work, and there is lots of work left to do. But now is the time to celebrate a milestone moment: the drawings phase.

And this has been your heart's desire all along—God's work done in God's way, through your ministry. With the master planning process behind you, you can be confident that you have exercised both your faith and the wisdom God has given you to lead His people to Kingdom heights. It's time for the planning to begin!

Epilogue:

Pastor Bob's Hope

The process had not always been a smooth one but, six months later, the project team had reached a remarkable degree of unity. Together, they had gained real insight into First Presbyterian's financial realities, ministry vision, DNA, and target; had prioritized the most important goals for the next stretch of years; and had arrived at a common understanding of their physical plant needs. Most important, there was a sense of possibility, of enthusiasm, of hope.

In a few moments, the architect would offer the big reveal of the pretty pictures Bob had wanted for so long. Meeting with Tom in the pastor's office moments before the meeting began, Bob had glanced again at the drawings and paused to thank God for His faithfulness, guidance, and patience.

"You know," he mused to Tom and to the architect as they walked together down the hallway to the conference room, "I had no idea what was going to be involved in this process when I began it. When I found out ... well, let's just say that there have been more than a few moments I have wanted to bail completely." He laughed and shook his head.

"But to tell you the truth, I have never been more excited about ministry and about the future of a church than I am right now. I really believe that by God's grace, First Presbyterian's greatest days are ahead of her."

Pastor Bob smiled at his new friends and opened the door to the conference room.

Appendices

Appendix A

Practical Application

I have offered a lot of detail and processes in this book. Perhaps it would be helpful to see all of that applied in a real-life situation. The following is a fairly straightforward case study of a church going through a master planning process.

Master Planning Case Study

Church Name:	First Church
Total Attendance:	760
Weekend Services:	3 (want to go to 2)
Sale of Existing Facility:	$4,200,000
Bought new land:	$1,200,000 (sold an existing site)

First Church is relocating to their new site and has been blessed to sell their former campus. They have bought a new site and their net cash on hand is $3,000,000. Many people in the church think that this net cash should be more than ample to build whatever they want for the new campus.

After going through extensive visioning, target market study, and DNA analysis, they have determined that they would like to have a worship facility that will allow them to change their program from three services to two services. With an average weekly attendance of 760, they would need to plan on a worship space that can seat about 800.

A good rule of thumb is that you design your new worship space for twice your current attendance. We assume that their current three services each has the same attendance, and when they change to two services, the attendance will be split equally as well. At an average weekly attendance of 760, each of the two new services will have 380 people in attendance before attendance grows (the goal of expansion of the ministry). Using two as the growth factor, we come in at just under 800 seats. Most church growth "experts" will say that when you are at 80 percent capacity, you will feel full. Hoping that the ministry will grow by a factor of two in the new space, even a large sanctuary of 800 seats will start to feel full if attendance reaches 640 per service (total attendance in worship of 1280 in the two services).

First Church has determined that it needs a worship space of 800 seats. So how much net usable space will this require? Design professionals will use ratios ranging from ten square feet per person to over fifteen square feet per person as part of the planning process. Each of these is derived using varying criteria and assumptions. This example uses fifteen square feet per person, which should be adequate for the congregational seating, proportionally sized platform, and backstage (baptismal, dressing, storage) space. The relevant equations show a need for about 12,000 square feet[1] of net usable square feet. (Note: Footnotes correspond to the worksheet in Appendix B; see note at end of this appendix for more information.)

First Church is a social church; the congregation likes to meet and greet both before and after services. They also want to have a welcome center, information kiosk, and informational displays, all of which should be housed in a main gathering lobby. Because they run two services, First Church will also need a logical traffic pattern for the crowd to navigate the communal areas between the two services. (The "turn" time between services can play a big role in the size of the foyer, narthex, or other gathering space, as well as size and location of the parking structure and the restrooms.) The most common ratio used by professionals for this space is between one and three square feet per person. In this instance, First Church intends to allow for thirty minutes between services, so the pressure on this space will be reduced some. In light of that, calculations based on two square feet per person are reasonable, and yield a total of 1,600 square feet[2].

As part of the extensive discovery process, ministry leaders realized that they have need for on-site classrooms. They need to accommodate children, youth, and some adult classes, with some of these running concurrently with the worship services. Given their programmatic needs, we have established that they need functional space at fifteen square feet per person. This will equate to 12,000 square feet[3].

In studying the church staff's collective DNA, it became clear that they enjoy working in a fairly close environment that encourages collaboration and interaction. They currently have what is considered an average of one pastoral staff person for every 100–150 people in the congregation, plus support staff. Given the current staffing, and figuring there will logically be some growth, we determined that the church should plan for twelve workspaces at an average size of twelve by fifteen feet (180 square feet per work area). This would indicate that they would need another 2,160 square feet[4].

First Church also has an active sports ministry, and they *love* to eat together as a church body. To accommodate these two elements of their church DNA, they would really like to have a full-court gymnasium, and a kitchen large enough to prepare large meals. A full-size gym, with adequate out of bounds and spectator areas requires 7,000 square feet[5a]; however, in a pinch, they could go with a half court at 3,500 square feet[5b]. Commercial kitchens will typically run 500–900 square feet. Given their affinity for fellowship, the larger version would be ideal[5c].

How about parking? The code requires a minimum four-to-one parking ratio. First Church has done their own parking analysis and has determined that they need a ratio of just two-and-a-quarter to one. With 800 seats, they will need 356 parking spaces. A typical stall (not including the handicap stalls) is 180 square feet, which translates to a need of 64,080 square feet for the parking spaces. As a rule of thumb, however, professionals suggest doubling that space in order to accommodate the drive aisles, turning radii, driveways, and other paved areas. This would increase the impervious conditions to 128,160 square feet[6], or about three acres of parking and pavement. As you can see, it takes a lot of land when you start including all the site improvements.

Here is a recap of the project square footage:

Worship Space[1]	=	12,000 SF
Foyer[2]	=	1,600 SF
Classrooms[3]	=	12,000 SF
Administration[4]	=	2,160 SF
Gymnasium/Fellowship[5a or 5b]	=	7,000 SF
Kitchen[5c]	=	900 SF

Total Dedicated/ Net Usable Square Footage = ┌─────────────┐ 35,660 SF └─────────────┘

Grossing Factor = ┌─────────────┐ X 1.25 └─────────────┘
(circulation, restrooms, electrical,
mechanical, storage)

Total Estimated Facility Square Footage Needed = ┌─────────────┐ 44,575 SF └─────────────┘

The question now is CAN THEY AFFORD IT? That is a topic for another discussion.

NOTE: Footnote numbers represent a guide to the location of data on the form in Appendix B.

Appendix B

Master Planning Case Study for Your Church

1. Sanctuary /Auditorium:

Requires 15 SF per person
Example: 800 seats x 15 SF = 12,000
This allows practical seating aisles and space for a large platform.
If there are special needs (perhaps for dramatic productions or and large presentations), use 16–18 SF per person.
Notes:

_____

_____

_____

Calculations: _____ seats x 15 SF per seat = | _____ SF
| (1)

2. Foyer:

The main foyer is being used in many churches for classes, displays, information, and fellowship. We recommend a minimum of 2 SF per person be allocated to the foyer.
Example: 800 seats x 2 = 1,600 SF
Notes:

_____

_____

_____

Calculations: _____ seats x 2 SF per person = | _____ SF
| (2)

3. **Classrooms:**

Individual spaces:

Nursery, ages birth to 2 years old: use 35 SF per child

Ages 3 through 5: use 35 SF per child

Ages 6 through 8: use 30 SF per child

Grades 3 through 12: use 25 SF per child

College through all adult classes: use 15 SF per person

General: A broader calculation of 15 SF per sanctuary/ auditorium seat will provide the total square footage needed for classrooms.

Example: 800 seats would require 12,000 SF (assuming no multiple use of classrooms)

Notes:

_____

_____

_____

Calculations: _____ seats x 15 SF per seat =

_____ SF
(3)

4. **Administration:**

Individual spaces in this category would be: Offices, secretary, work area, conference rooms, resource library

General: An average size of 12 x 15 (180 SF) can be used for each individual space

Example: 12 spaces (7 offices, 1 workroom, 1 secretary, 2 conference rooms and 1 resource library) would require 2,160 SF

Notes:

_____

_____

_____

Calculations: _____ spaces x 180 SF per space =

_____ SF
(4)

5. Gymnasium/Fellowship Hall:

If the church desires a full size gymnasium, the size for a gym floor area is generally 70 x 100, or 7,000, SF.

Most church kitchens should be 500 SF–900 SF to accommodate the number of volunteer staff that may be serving in the kitchen during a banquet or other function.

Notes:

_____

_____

_____

Calculations:

Full Size Gym/Fellowship Hall: 7,000 SF =

_____ SF
(5a)

Half Court Gym/Fellowship Hall: 3,500 SF =

_____ SF
(5b)

Kitchen Area =

_____ SF
(5c)

6. Parking:

Ideal requirement is a ratio of one stall for every 2.25 seats in Sanctuary/Auditorium

Example: 800-seat sanctuary requires 356 parking stalls. Many local jurisdictions require one (1) stall for every 3–4 seats, but this is not a practical ratio.

Notes:

_____

_____

_____

Calculations: _____ seats / 2.25 spaces per seat

= _____ parking stalls, _____ parking

Stalls x 180 SF per stall x 200 (aisles) = | _____ SF
                                            | *(6)*

7. Total Square Footage of Facility:

Sanctuary/Auditorium	_____ SF *(1)*
Foyer	_____ SF *(2)*
Classrooms	_____ SF *(3)*
Administration	_____ SF *(4)*
Gymnasium/Fellowship Hall	_____ SF *(5a or 5b)*
Kitchen Area	_____ SF *(5c)*
Total Usable/Programmable Area Square Footage	_____ SF
Circulation, Restrooms, Electrical, HVAC, Storage (25% of usable/programmable SF)	X 1.25
Total Estimated Facility Square Footage Needed	_____ SF *(7)*

About the Author

Tim Cool, President & CSO (Chief Solutions Officer),
Cool Solutions Group

Since 1986, Tim has assisted more than two hundred churches and ministry organizations throughout the United States with their facilities. While employed by a national church building organization, Tim collaborated with the Christian community in the areas of facility needs analysis, design coordination, and consultation. As projects progressed, Tim coordinated the site and property analysis, team integration and leadership, financing and construction. Tim has a thorough knowledge of facilities and their systems.

Tim has also been a conference speaker at numerous national conferences and seminars. He teaches on topics of interest to growing churches, particularly the impact the physical facility has on the organization. His experience and expertise make him one of the most sought-after experts in church/ministry organization development and processes.

He maintains his national membership with the International Code Council for building codes. He is also a member of the National Association of Church Business Administrators, National Association of Church Facility Managers and the International Facilities Managers Association. Tim has been an active member of C12 (Christian Business Organization) for more than four years and is a member of Elevation Church in Charlotte, NC.

Tim has been married to his best friend, Lisa, for twenty-five years, and resides in Charlotte, NC with their thirteen-year-old triplets. In his spare time, Tim enjoys playing the trumpet, vacationing in the mountains, and doodling on several social networks. You can contact Tim Cool directly at info@coolsolutionsgroup.com or on the web at www.coolsolutionsgroup.com

Endnotes

1   ^Sara N Martin, *Site Assessment and Remediation Handbook*, CRC Press (2003)

2   ^Thomas M Missimer and Missimer M Missimer, *A Lender's Guide to Environmental Liability Management* CRC Press (1996)

3   ^*Environmental Aspects of Real Estate and Commercial Transactions: From Brownfields to Green Buildings*, American Bar Association, ed. By James B. Witkin (2002)

4   Source: http://www.appleseeds.org/noah_today.htm